Hello!
I am an ape.

I0115150

There are two types of apes...

Well, that's great!

...Great apes...

Sometimes less is more.

... and Lesser apes

Great apes include chimpanzees, bonobos, gorillas and orangutans.

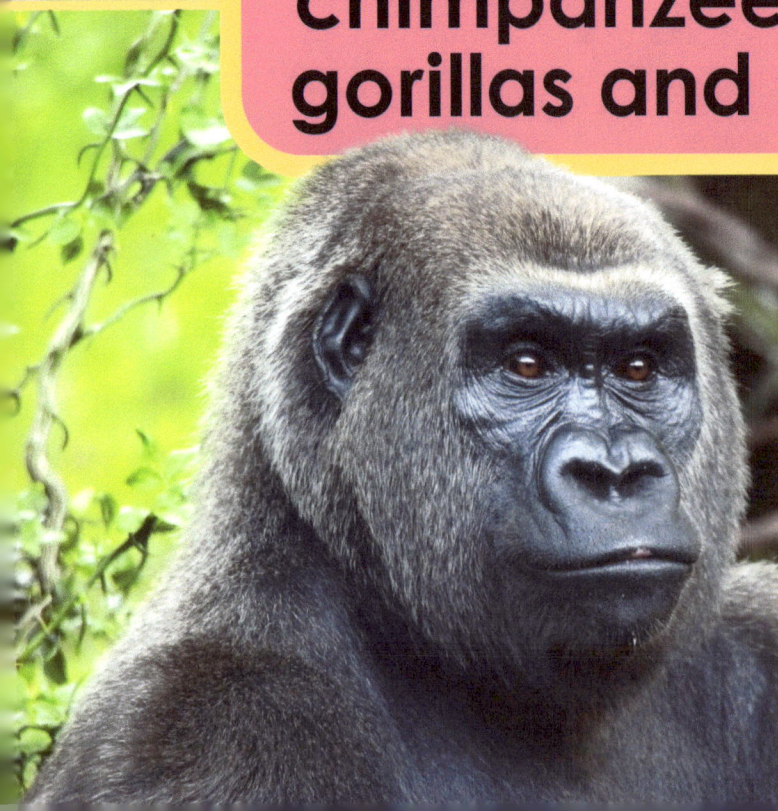

Lesser apes include siamangs and gibbons.

The biggest ape is the male gorilla.

I can weigh up to 400 pounds (180kg).

I'm 6 times as strong as a human.

Apes are very intelligent and can learn to use tools.

What tools can you use?

Who needs a tail anyway?

Great apes don't have tails.

Apes are mainly "arboreal".

That means we love living life in the trees.

Gibbons are excellent acrobats with great balance.

I can walk, climb, jump and swing through the trees.

Gorillas live in family groups.

I'm in charge!

The leader of the gorilla family is the silverback male.

Siamangs have a large "throat sac".

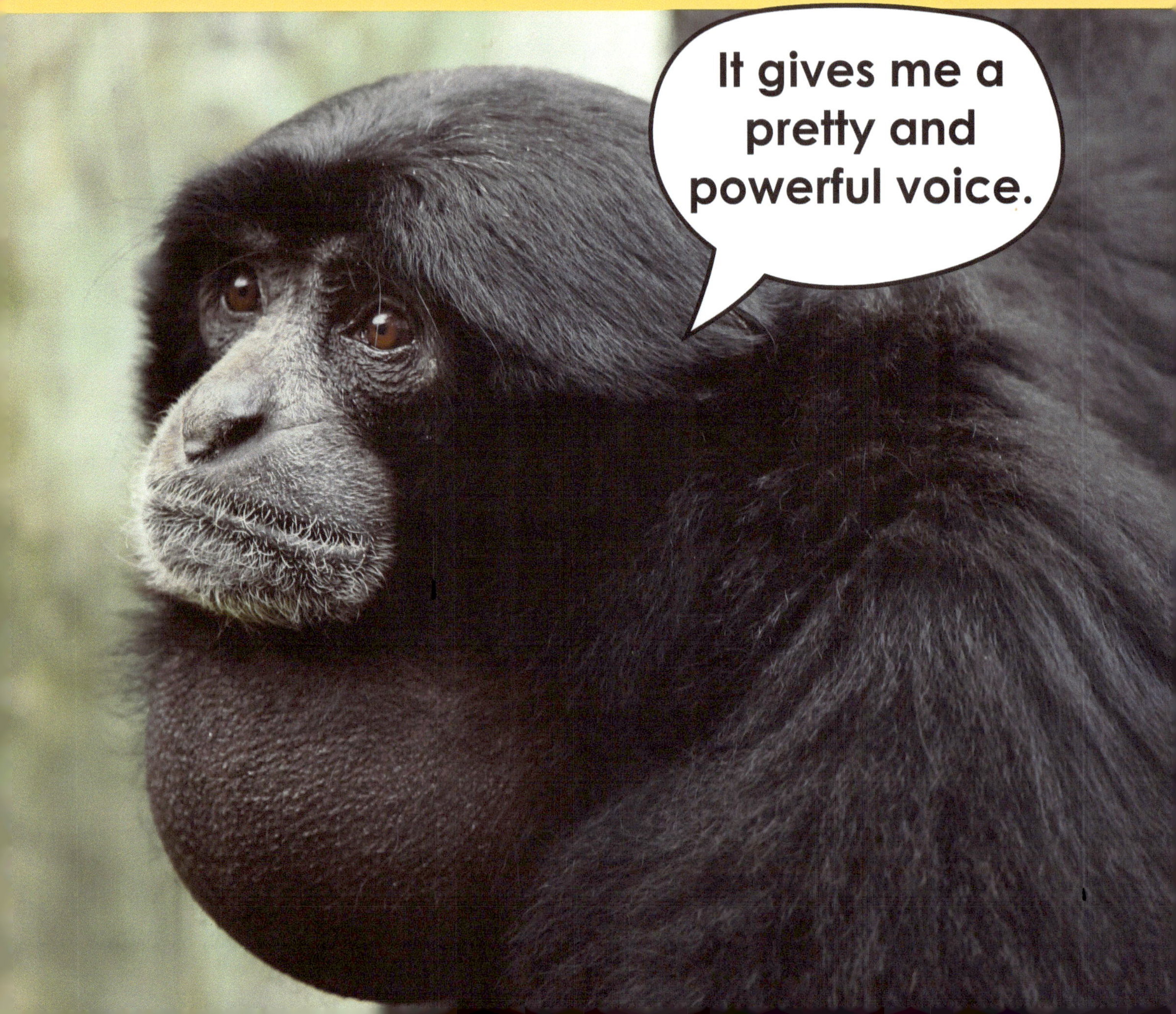

Siamangs' loud call has a melody, so its called a "song".

The word "orangutan" is from the Malay words "orang hutan," which mean "person of the forest."

Orangutans are excellent climbers and can easily move through the forest.

Gorillas are "herbivores", so they don't eat meat.

I mainly eat leaves, stems and fruits.

Other apes are "omnivores", so they sometimes eat insects and meat.

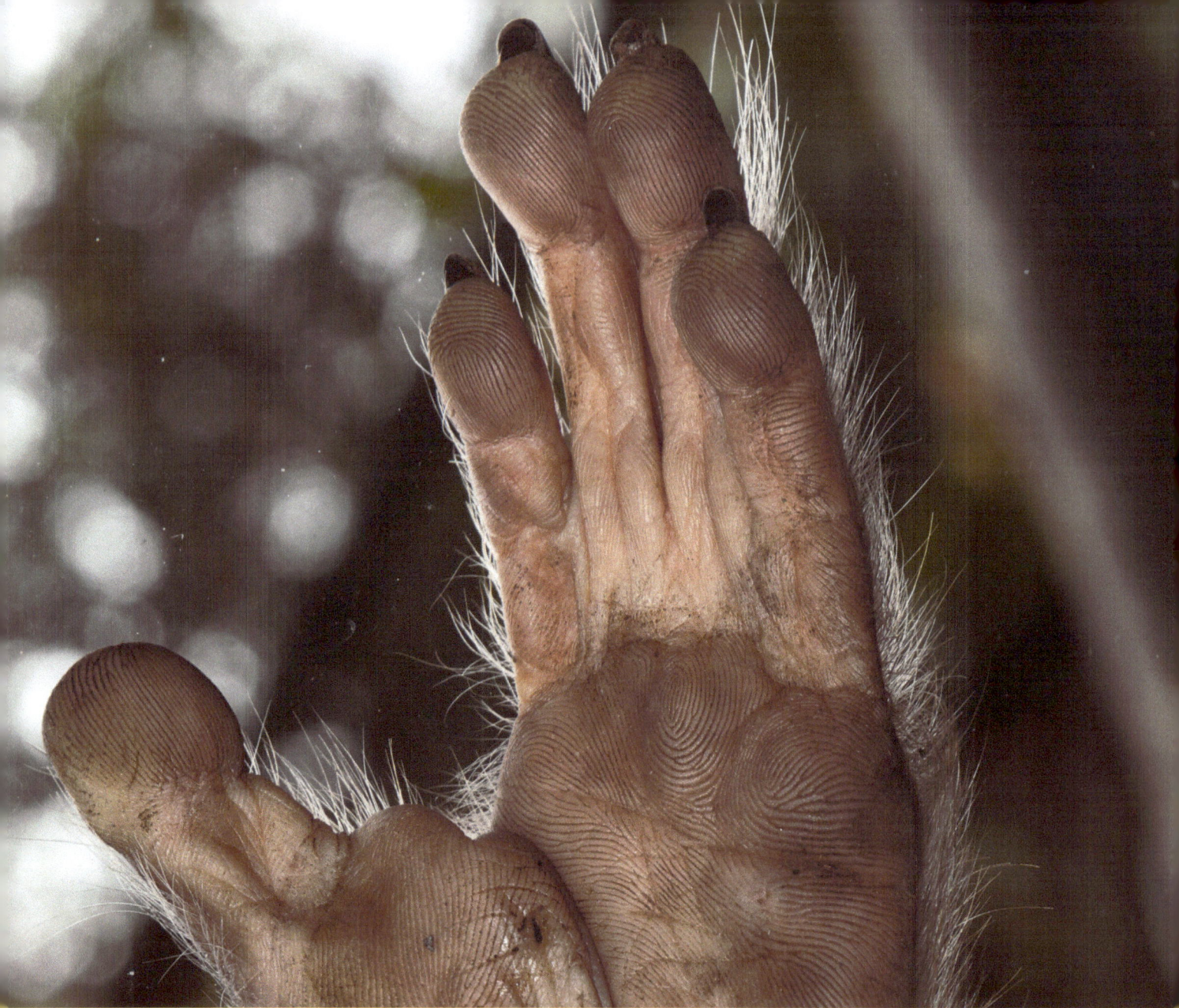

Each ape has a unique fingerprint, just like humans.

A group of gorillas is called a "troop".

Feeling good!

Apes have a variety of facial expressions, including smiles, frowns, and gestures, to communicate with each other.

Just like humans, we all have different expressions and emotions.

Apes have strong family connections.

Mothers take care of and protect their children.

Hang on, dear.

Apes have complex relationships.
Sometimes groups even go to war.

After a fight, apes might make up by grooming or hugging each other.

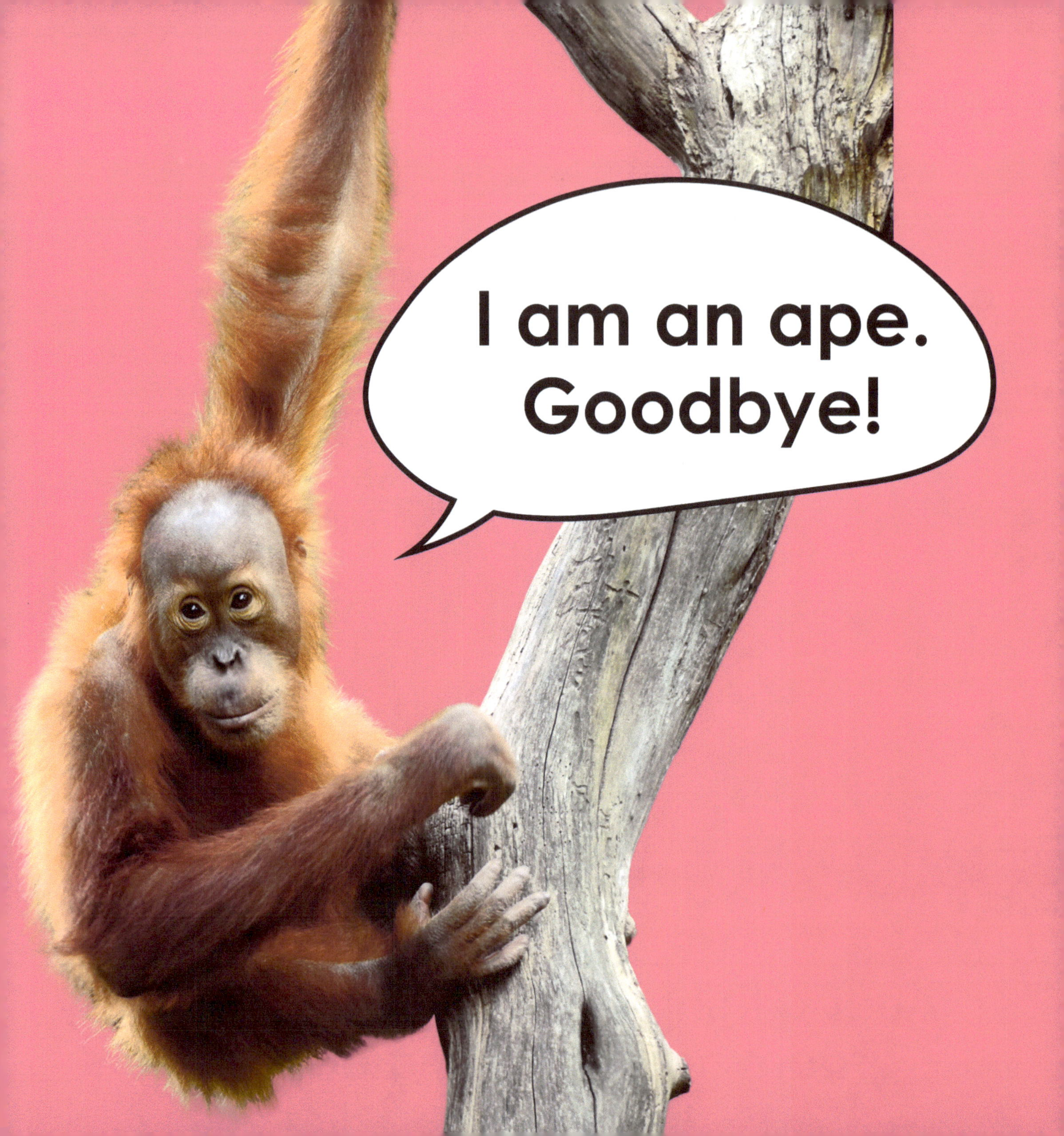
I am an ape.
Goodbye!

Hello parents!

scan here

Visit us to find out about new releases and *FREE* offers. We'll let you know when we have a new release coming out and how you can get it for FREE.
And you can cast your vote for what book we make next!

ActiveBrainsBooks.com

or visit here

scan here

Let us know what you think. As an independent publisher, your honest reviews mean a lot to us and our business. We'd love to hear from you!

amazon.com/review/create-review/

or visit here

FOLLOW US on Amazon.

amazon.com/author/activebrainsbooks

ActiveBrainsBooks.com

ACTIVE BRAINS

www.ingramcontent.com/pod-product-compliance
Lightning Source LLC
Chambersburg PA
CBHW060845270326
41933CB00003B/197